Materials

Wood

Cassie Mayer

Heinemann
LIBRARY

www.heinemann.co.uk/library
Visit our website to find out more information about Heinemann Library books.

To order:
 Phone 44 (0) 1865 888066
 Send a fax to 44 (0) 1865 314091
 Visit the Heinemann Bookshop at www.heinemann.co.uk/library to browse our catalogue and order online.

First published in Great Britain by Heinemann Library, Halley Court, Jordan Hill, Oxford OX2 8EJ, part of Pearson Education. Heinemann is a registered trademark of Pearson Education Ltd.

Editorial: Diyan Leake
Design: Joanna Hinton-Malivoire
Picture research: Tracy Cummins and Heather Mauldin
Production: Duncan Gilbert

Originated by Chroma Graphics (Overseas) Pte Ltd
Printed and bound in China by South China Printing Co. Ltd

ISBN 978 0 431 19264 2
12 11 10 09 08
10 9 8 7 6 5 4 3 2 1

British Library Cataloguing in Publication Data
Mayer, Cassie
  Wood. - (Materials)
  1. Wood - Juvenile literature
  I. Title
  620.1'2

Acknowledgments
The author and publisher are grateful to the following for permission to reproduce copyright material: © Corbis pp. **5** (Kevin Fleming), **20** (Brand X); © Heinemann Raintree pp. **6**, **9**, **10**, **11**, **12**, **13**, **15**, **16**, **17**, **21**, **22** bottom left, **22** bottom right, **23** bottom, **23** top (David Rigg); © istockphoto pp. **18**, **22** top right (Michael Braun); © Shutterstock pp. **4** (Elena Elisseeva), **7** (Olga Zaporozhskaya), **8** (Mikhail Olykainen), **19** (Semen Lixodeev), **22** top right (Olga Zaporozhskaya), **23** middle (Elena Elisseeva).

Cover image used with permission of © Getty Images (Chuck Kuhn Photography, Inc.). Back cover image used with permission of © istockphoto (Michael Braun).

Every effort has been made to contact copyright holders of any material reproduced in this book. Any omissions will be rectified in subsequent printings if notice is given to the publisher.

12. FEB 15.

08. FEB 18.

RBWM LIBRARY SERVICES

38067100384371

Please return/renew this item by the last date shown. Books may also be renewed by phone or Internet.

 www.rbwm.gov.uk/web/libraries.htm

C ☎ 01628 796969 (library hours)

 ☎ 0303 123 0035 (24 hours)

The Royal Borough
Windsor &
Maidenhead

Contents

What is wood?

Wood is a natural material.
It is found in the world around us.

4

Wood is from trees.

Wood can be hard.

Wood can be smooth.

Some wood is heavy.

Some wood is light.

What happens when wood is set on fire?

Wood burns when it is set on fire.

Flames make the wood burn.

Burning wood makes light and heat.

A powder called ash is left when wood burns.

How does water change wood?

Water can change wood.

Wood changes if it is in water for a long time.

Wet wood can become soft.

If wood is wet and soft, we say it is rotten.

How do people use wood?

Wood can be used to make buildings.

Wood can be used to make paper.

Wood can be used to make fires in our homes.

Wood can be used to make lots
of things.

Things made of wood

▲ houses

▲ tables and chairs

▲ sculptures

▲ paper

Picture glossary

natural in the world around us. Plants, animals, rocks, water, and soil are part of the natural world.

powder very tiny pieces of soft, dry stuff

rotten broken down by water

Content vocabulary for teachers

material something that can be used to make things

Index

Notes for parents and teachers

Before reading   Put items made of materials such as wood, plastic, metal, rock, and rubber in a closed bag. Challenge the children to feel in the bag and, without looking, identify the object made of wood. What does it feel like? Is it cold to touch? Is it heavy? Talk about the properties of wood. Ask the children where we get wood from and talk about trees and forests.

After reading

• Show children different examples of wood – dark wood such as mahogany, light wood such as beech, red wood such as cherry. Encourage them to describe the colour of the wood and the effect of the grain.

• Play "I Spy". Challenge the children to think of something made of wood and to give the rest of the group the starting letter. For example, "I spy with my little eye something made of wood beginning with 'd'" [door].

Picture glossary

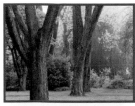

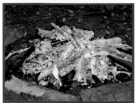

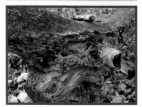